This is a photographic journal of an actual Osprey family in the summer of 2012. Their nest was located on Scotch Bonnet tributary behind the Wetlands Institute in Stone Harbor, NJ.

It's a story about Homer, the youngest of three chicks, and his struggle to learn to fly like his older brother and sister.

DEDICATION

Dedicated to Joanne, my wife of 58 years. As my Chief Bird Spotter, I credit her for many of the photographs in this book.

HOMER'S STORY

This is the story of Homer the Osprey. Osprey?…what a strange name! What is an osprey?

An osprey is a large bird some people mistake for an eagle. Have you ever seen an osprey? Have you ever seen an eagle?

This is an Osprey

This is an Eagle

Can you see the difference?

Homer was born in the Wetlands near Stone Harbor, New Jersey in the Spring of 2012. Homer's mother, Gertrude, produced three eggs with her mate for life, Maurice. Homer was the last egg to be laid by Gertrude.

The first egg to hatch was Homer's big brother, Hercules. The next egg to hatch was Homer's sister, Henrietta. Homer was the last egg to hatch. He was the smallest of the new family.

Very young osprey chicks are not beautiful but get cuter as they grow older.

Here's a closeup of Hercules when he was very young. Do you think he is cute?

As the chicks grew, Maurice and Gertrude had to work very hard to catch the six pounds of fish needed to feed the family each day. Hercules was growing much faster than Henrietta, and Henrietta was growing much faster than Homer.

Here's Gertrude trying to feed Homer. You can barely see him behind Hercules, as Henrietta looks on, but…

…Hercules nudged Homer out of the way and got fed instead of Homer. No wonder Hercules was growing so fast!

Ospreys have excellent eyesight and are great fishers. It's a good thing because osprey chicks are ALWAYS hungry.

This is Maurice bringing back a fish he caught in the wetlands.
When fish are caught, they wiggle and squirm and try to get away. Many times ospreys bite off the fish's head so they can bring the fish back to the nest.

When Maurice got back to the nest with the fish, he bit off pieces and gave them to Gertrude. She chewed them up and then fed the bits to the chicks.

Here's Gertrude feeding Hercules. Notice the color of Hercules' eyes. When ospreys are young, their eyes are orangey. When they get older their eye color will change to more of a golden-yellow, like Gertrude's are in the picture.

Osprey parents are very protective of their chicks from predators such as seagulls, eagles or even owls.

Gertrude screams at a predator seagull as Hercules, Henrietta and Homer huddle close to the nest.

Gertrude
then flaps
her wings
to chase
away the
gull.

It wasn't too long before the chicks no longer had to be fed
and were eating on their own. Below you can see Hercules
eating while Henrietta watches.

Soon Hercules was strong enough to flap his wings the same way Maurice and Gertrude do.

As Henrietta watches he flaps his wings even harder...

...and lifts himself off the nest.

HERCULES IS READY
TO FLY!!

Soon he took off
from the nest as
Homer watched.

After flying over the
wetlands Hercules
returns to the nest
with a perfect
landing on the post.

Very soon after Hercules was flying, Henrietta also learned to fly…Homer sat and watched.

As much as he tried, Homer still couldn't fly.

Hercules looked at
Homer as if to say,
"Why aren't you
trying to fly?"...

...so
Homer
tried while
Hercules
watched.

Homer kept
trying, but
Hercules lost
interest and
turned the
other way.

Henrietta and Hercules wondered if Homer would ever fly.

Even his mother looked down at Homer as if to say, "Homer, you must try harder. Hercules and Henrietta are already flying and catching fish for the family to eat."

Homer tried and tried while his mother watched but still couldn't fly.

Finally, Homer looked up at his mother as if to say, "Gee mom, I'm trying my best!"

Homer felt bad that he had disappointed the family especially his mom whom he loved so much.

Then one day all the family left the nest to catch fish. Homer was left alone.

So he started flapping his wings....

...and jumping...

....and
jumping even
higher!

Soon he
could feel the
wind beneath
his wings!

He went to the edge
of the nest and
flapped his wings as
hard as he could…

…and jumped
off into the wind!
HOMER WAS
FLYING!!

Flapping his wings
harder and harder…

…he looked around
and thought, "This is
hard work, but I
know I can do it!."

And he did! He spread his
wings and soared high into
the sky….

....and then flew down toward the ground....

....and over two egrets feeding in the wetlands.

Flying was becoming easier and easier. It was a feeling of freedom he had never known before!

As he flew
over the nest
he looked
down and saw
his dad with
Hercules who
was looking
up at him.

Hercules turned to
his father as if to say,
"You won't believe
what I just saw! It
was Homer flying
just above us!"

Homer soared through the air, but he was getting tired and knew he had to get back to the nest.

To do this he would have to make his first attempt at landing.

After circling the nest several times he tried to land on top of one of the posts…

...but his foot hit the back of the post. He couldn't stop.

Spreading his wings to slow himself down, he put his feet out in front of him...

...and landed on the same corner of the nest from where he took off. He was so proud of himself and knew how pleased his family would be that he could now fly.

Now that Homer was flying, it was time for Maurice and Gertrude to teach him to catch fish. They took him over the wetlands and showed him how to spot fish just under the surface of the water.

Homer learned quickly and became very good at catching fish. Here's Homer landing on the nest with his first fish. How do you think Homer felt about his first catch?

His proud mom squawked at the others to get their attention so they could see the fish that Homer caught.

Now all the family was flying and fishing and having a wonderful summer. Gertrude looked at Hercules, Henrietta and Homer. They knew how very proud she was of them.

Soon winter would come and the family would have to prepare to travel many miles to warmer weather. They would fly all the way to South America where Maurice and Gertrude spent every winter since they have been together.

It's possible that not everyone would survive the long trip to South America and back to Stone Harbor next spring. Hopefully, Homer and his siblings will find mates and return next year with Maurice and Gertrude to raise many more beautiful ospreys.

Homer was now a very proud osprey.

THE END

ADDENDUM

The wetlands near Stone Harbor, New Jersey have many species of birds feeding in the area.

There are American Oystercatchers feeding on the banks....

….and flying overhead.

Cormorants drying their wings....

….and skimming along the water.

Great Egrets wading
along the banks
looking for small fish….

….and flying gracefully
over the wetland grass.

Tri-colored herons
looking for a meal….

….and Little Blue Herons
taking flight.

This is a great great place to live, visit, AND take pictures!
Come see us sometime.

<u>SOME FACTS ABOUT OSPREYS</u>

Ospreys mate for life. Their nest (built by both sexes) is a bulky pile of sticks lined with smaller materials such as marsh grass. Ospreys may use the same nest for years, adding material each year, so that the nest becomes huge.

 The female will lay 2-4 eggs in the spring. They produce only one brood each year. Both parents take turns sitting on the eggs during the incubation period, but the female does most of the sitting while the male hunts for food.

The eggs will then take about 5 weeks to hatch. Osprey eggs don't hatch all at once but are staggered in time so that some siblings are older and more dominant. When food is scarce these stronger birds may take it all and leave their siblings to starve. When osprey chicks are born, they are tiny and very vulnerable. During the early stages many osprey chicks are eaten by birds ospreys compete with. These generally include members of the Owl Species like the Great Horned Owl and eagles like the Golden Eagle and the Bald Eagle.

The female remains with young most of the time at first, sheltering them from sun and rain and protecting them from predators. As the male brings back fish, the female feeds them to the young. Age of young at first flight averages about 51-54 days.

Their diet consists almost entirely of fish. Ospreys will rarely eat small mammals, birds, or reptiles, and only when fish are scarce. Ospreys have very good eyesight that is particularly good at spotting fish under the surface of the water and are highly attuned to movement. Ospreys hunt by diving to the water's surface from some 30 to 100 feet up.

Birds that ospreys compete with are numerous, so the osprey must be ahead of the game in order to be successful. The osprey has many modifications to help it to hunt. Many of these modifications are what set the osprey apart from all other birds of prey. First, the osprey has equal toe lengths. Every other diurnal bird of prey has unequal toe lengths. Secondly, ospreys are the only diurnal raptor to have a reversible outer toe which they can swivel backwards to aid in gripping slippery fish! Ospreys also have rounded talons which are hooked to grip fish. Their feet are large and powerful; ospreys also have relatively long legs for grabbing fish under the surface of the water.

The Osprey Bird species have long broad wings not unlike the eagles. These powerful wings help them to get airborne again after catching a large fish. In flight, ospreys will orient the fish headfirst to ease wind resistance. Many times they will bite the fish's head off before bringing it back to the nest.

An osprey sometimes finds it very hard to drop a fish that it has caught due to its curved talons. If it grabs a fish that is too heavy, it cannot take off from the water and sometimes cannot let go. This inevitably leads to the drowning of the osprey.

North American osprey population became endangered in the 1950's due to chemical pollutants such as DDT which thinned their eggshells and hampered reproduction. Ospreys have rebounded significantly in recent decades, though they remain scarce in some locales. Most ospreys are migratory birds that breed in the north and migrate south for the winter.

www.ingramcontent.com/pod-product-compliance
Lightning Source LLC
Chambersburg PA
CBHW040036240726
48664CB00003B/952